The Astonishing Armadillo

The Astonishing Armadillo

by Dee Stuart

A Carolrhoda Nature Watch Book

Carolrhoda Books, Inc./Minneapolis

For Aubrey, Ardis, and William, with love.

Thanks to Dr. Eleanor Storrs Burchfield, Florida Institute of Technology, and to Jim Dunlap for their assistance with this book.

This book is available in two editions:
Library binding by Carolrhoda Books, Inc.
Soft cover by First Avenue Editions
c/o The Lerner Group
241 First Avenue North
Minneapolis, MN 55401

LIBRARY OF CONGRESS CATALOGING-IN-PUBLICATION DATA

Stuart, Dee.
The astonishing armadillo / by Dee Stuart.
p. cm.
"A Carolrhoda nature watch book."
Includes index.
Summary: Describes the physical characteristics, habitat, and life cycle of the armadillo.
ISBN 0-87614-769-4 (lib. bdg.)
ISBN 0-87614-630-2 (pbk.)
1. Armadillos—Juvenile literature. [1. Armadillos.] I. Title.
QL737.E23S78 1993
599.3′1—dc20 92-25970
CIP
AC

Manufactured in the United States of America

2 3 4 5 6 98 97 96 95 94

A nine-banded armadillo (Dasypus novemcinctus)

Slowly, slowly, for the past 150 years, a small army has trundled steadily northward from Mexico. In 1854 the army crossed the Mexican border and invaded Texas. The invaders were small creatures, each with a head like a lizard's, eyes like a pig's, ears like a mule's, a snout like a hog's, claws like a bear's, and a tail like a rat's. These astonishing creatures were nine-banded armadillos. Naturalist John James Audubon described the armadillo as "a small pig in the shell of a turtle."

Armadillos, with their natural armor, are unique among mammals. The shoulders and rump, legs, top of head, and tail of the armadillo are encased in a **carapace,** or bony shell, made up of large brownish plates or shields. Only the soft, leathery belly is unprotected. These overlapping shields are covered with a leathery skin unlike the hard shell of a turtle. Between the shoulders and the rump are (usually) 8 to 11 bony bands that protect the back and sides. The bands are connected by folds in the skin so that the armadillo can bend its body like an accordion. Early Spanish explorers thought the animal's bony shield resembled their own armor and named it armadillo, or "little armored one." This tough armor has helped "nature's little tank" to survive for 55 million years. Scientists today believe armadillos may be mini-dinosaurs, relatives of the glyptodont, a giant armadillo-like animal of prehistoric times.

The nine-banded armadillo is the only member of the armadillo family found in the United States. It is closely related to the armadillos, anteaters, and tree sloths of Central and South America. All belong to the scientific order or group called **edentates,** which means "without teeth." But only the anteaters have no teeth. Most armadillos have seven or eight small, peg-shaped molars on each side of their upper and lower jaws that they use to crush their food.

Armadillos vary in color. They can be many shades of beige, brownish gray, or dark brown to almost black. Sometimes their earthy coloring blends with their surroundings and makes it hard for their enemies to see them.

Although nine-banded armadillos feed mainly on insects, they also take in a small amount of roots, dirt, and debris, which helps them digest their food and keeps their teeth from growing too long. Though they prefer beetles, ants, and termites, they also eat earthworms, caterpillars, toads, small snakes and frogs, lizards, roaches, scorpions, millipedes, centipedes, or even dead birds if they appear in the animals' path. They like to visit drying ponds, where they fish for shrimp, small crayfish, stranded minnows, and **larvae** (the wiggly, worm-like young of insects).

Armadillos have been accused of eating the eggs of ground-nesting birds, digging up grains, and destroying melon and tomato crops. But research shows that wild armadillos have little interest in birds' eggs. Their peg-like teeth are not good for gnawing, chewing, or cracking eggs. They are fond of **maggots** (the worm-like eggs of flies), and they will eat melons or soft fruits if the crop is overripe or has been split open. In Louisiana and Texas, they show a passion for fire ants.

Worms are among the favorite foods of armadillos.

Nine-banded armadillos probe for food in the ground (left) *and in the bark of a rotting log* (opposite page).

The armadillo is luckier than most mammals because it never has to stray far from home to find food. It rambles around in a random path or scuttles along a creek bank rooting through leaves and dirt for insects. Although it cannot see very clearly with its small pig eyes, or hear very well with its mule-like ears, it has an amazingly acute sense of smell. With its snout pressed to the ground, it can locate insects 6 to 8 inches (15-20 cm) deep in the dirt.

The armadillo's method of seeking food is called probing. It likes to probe in old decaying logs, at the base of bunch grasses, and in loose mixtures of clay, silt, and sandy soil.

It pushes its long snout through leaves and brush, then plows a furrow or trench about 3 to 4 inches (8-10 cm) deep through the dirt. Suddenly it starts digging furiously with its strong, sharp claws, then plunges its nose into the conical hole that it has dug. The armadillo's long, flicking, cylindrical tongue shoots out far beyond the end of its snout, where it may capture a tongueful of its favorite foods, such as crisp, crunchy black ants, beetles, or termites. How does the armadillo trap food? Its tongue is covered with sticky saliva and little wart-like projections. When its tongue shoots out, the insects stick to the wet, gooey surface. As the armadillo feeds, it makes a snuffling sound. If, nearby, a dog barks, the small creature, intent on its search, appears not to hear this warning of danger and continues probing for food.

Notice the long, sharp claws on this nine-banded armadillo's toes.

The armadillo has four toes on its forefeet and five toes on its hind feet. All are armed with large, strong claws. The middle two claws on the forefeet and the middle three on the back feet are longest. They make excellent tools for digging up insects, opening nests, and carving out burrows. Although armadillos can use their long, sharp claws for fighting, they are timid creatures and seldom do battle with enemies. Sometimes they emit a sharp, musky odor from a pair of glands located near the base of the tail. When these critters are on the move, their drooping tails leave trails that look like ropes running between a set of tracks.

Unlike most mammals, which have a sturdy coat of hair or fur, nine-banded armadillos have very little hair. Most of the hair they do have is on the soft underparts and is sparsely scattered on the shell.

The shaded area shows the range of the armadillo.

Nine-banded armadillos belong to the species known as *Dasypus novemcinctus* in the armadillo family Dasypodidae. The Dasypodidae family has about 20 species, or kinds, including the three-, six-, seven-, and eleven-banded armadillos and the pygmy, pichi, peludo, giant, and pink fairy armadillos. All of these cousins of the nine-banded armadillo live in Central and South America.

A six-banded armadillo—one of the nine-banded armadillo's South American cousins

The giant armadillo, whose scientific name is *Priodontes giganteus*, is 5 feet (1.5 m) long from snout to tail-tip, and weighs from about 99 to about 130 pounds (45-60 kg). It makes its home in Brazil. Although it has as many as one hundred teeth, the teeth are smaller than those of other armadillos. They are well suited to its diet, fine for crunching a meal of termites and a few ants. Its forefeet are also well suited to its diet, for the third toe is armed with a sickle-like claw used to tear rotten logs or to rip apart termite nests.

The smallest armadillo is the pink fairy, *Chalamyphorus truncatus*. Only 5 inches (12.7 cm) long and weighing about ⅓ pound (.14 kg), it lives underground in Argentina. A soft, pink shell with 23 to 25 bands covers its silken skin.

Nine-banded armadillos are about the size of big house cats. They average 2.5 feet (75 cm) in total length. The tapering tail, composed of 12 to 14 bony rings, is half as long as the body. Males and females look alike and are about the same size, although males can be slightly larger than females. Adult male and female nine-banded armadillos weigh from about 8 to about 15 pounds (3.6-6.8 kg).

Armadillos' main occupation is the search for food and water. Sometimes their endless search for these necessities leads them beyond their normal haunts, and they are unable to find their way home. Then they **migrate**, or move on, to a new area in search of the conditions they need to live. There they dig new dens and begin a new **colony,** or settlement, of armadillos.

For whatever reason, in the 1800s they continued their trek northward from Mexico in one of the fastest known migrations in the history of mammals. They first invaded the Rio Grande valley. Then, turning away from the dry western deserts, which offered them little life-giving water, they spread north to Kansas and Missouri. Other bands of armadillos shuffled slowly eastward toward Florida.

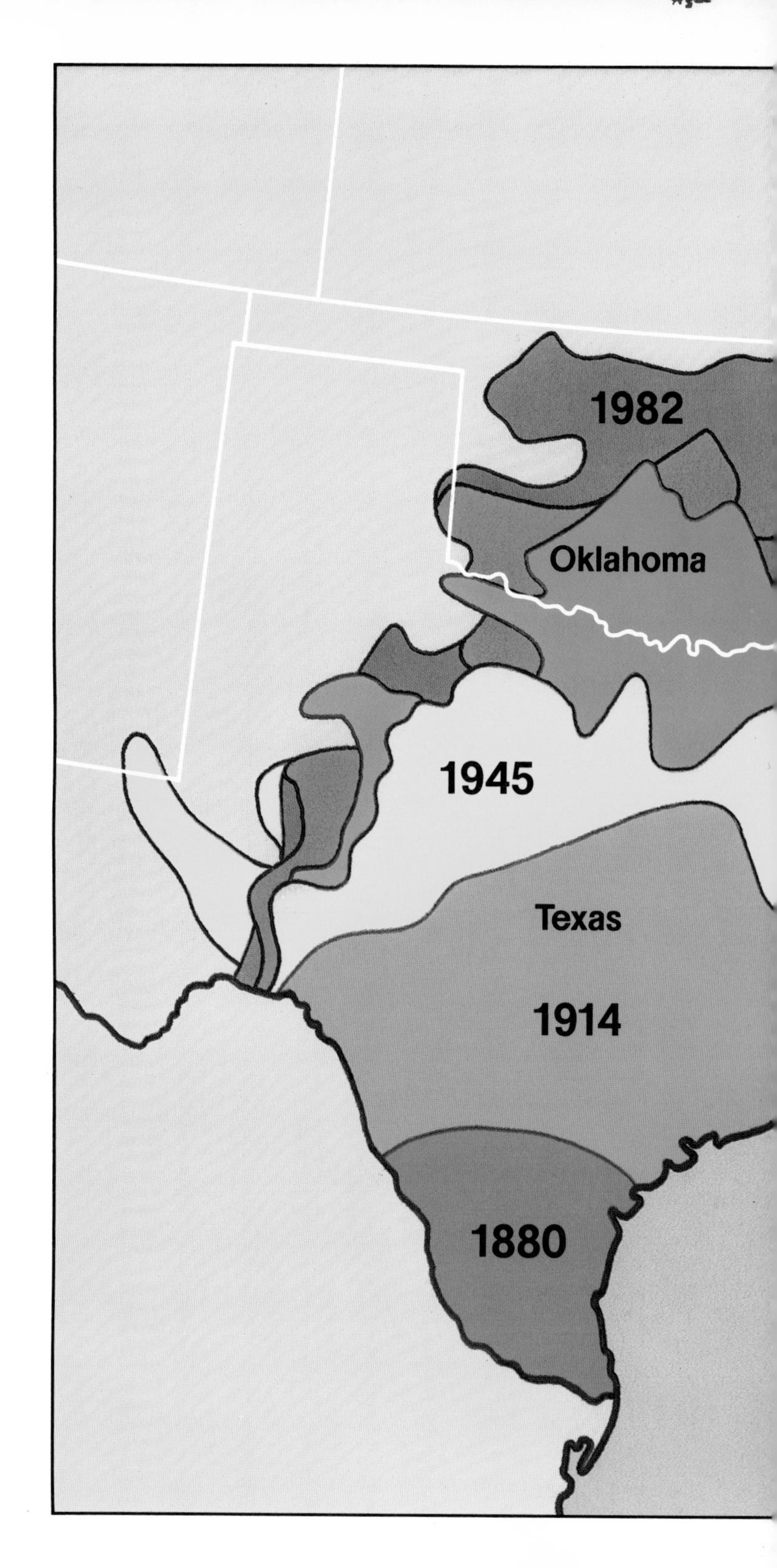

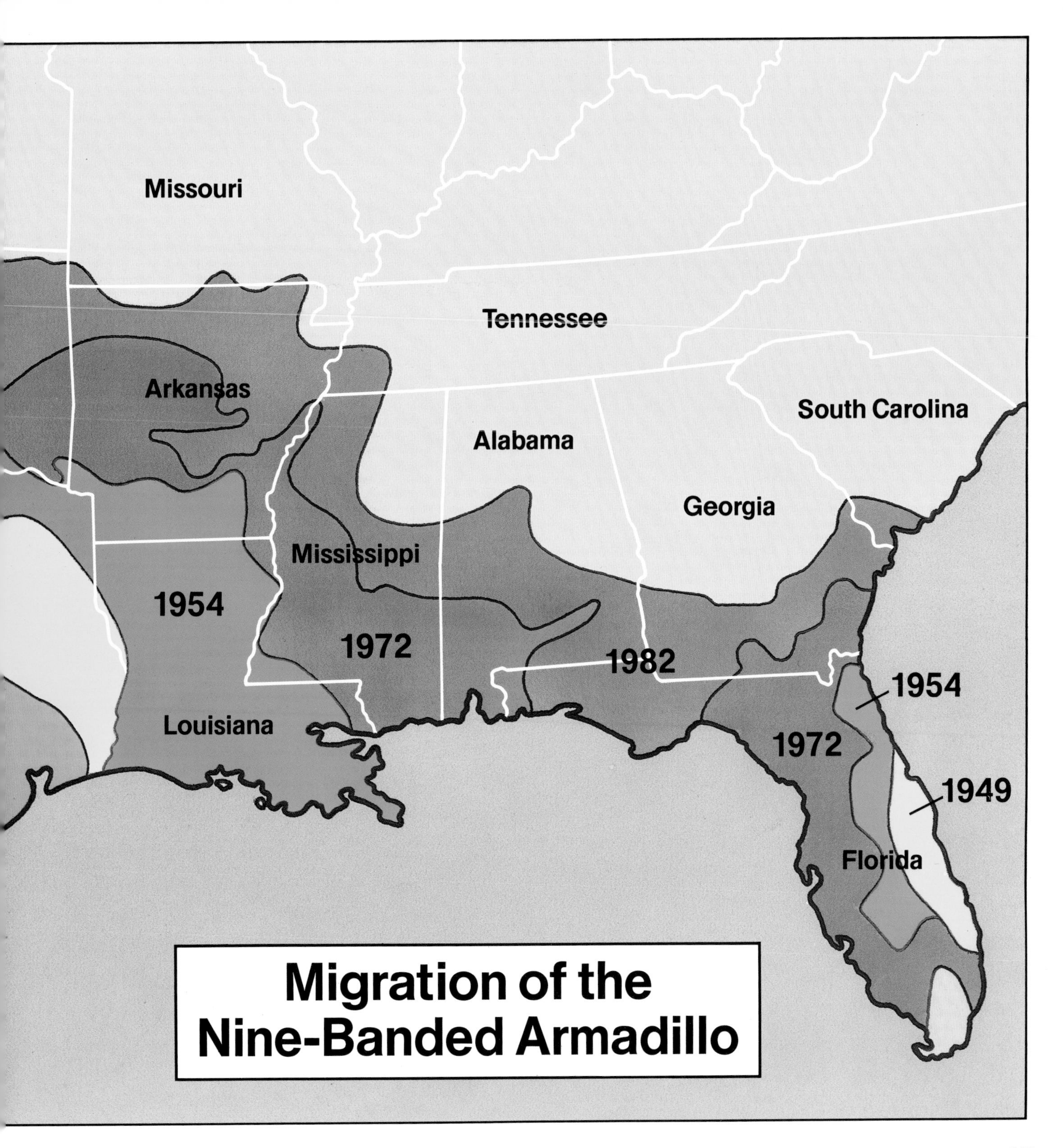
Missouri
Tennessee
Arkansas
South Carolina
Alabama
Georgia
Mississippi
1954
1972
1982
1954
Louisiana
1972
1949
Florida
Migration of the
Nine-Banded Armadillo

Water is usually not an obstacle for armadillos, who are good swimmers.

On the endless search for food, or a new home, an armadillo often comes face to face with a river, a lake, or a swift-running stream. Normally water is no obstacle to these unusual creatures, for they are excellent swimmers. Though the armadillo tends to sink in water, it has an astonishing hidden talent. To cross a body of water, it plunges in and gulps in air, which inflates its stomach and intestines like a balloon. It then paddles or floats across. More astonishing, if the small swimmer tires, it can sink to the bottom and cross underwater on foot. If alarmed, it can cross a stream faster than its usual dog-paddle speed by running across the bottom. It can stay underwater for up to 10 minutes. If a stream is not too deep or too wide, the armadillo will often walk across the bottom rather than swimming.

How these small pioneers managed to cross the great Mississippi River remains a mystery to this day. Some people think they may have floated across the river on driftwood, stowed away on boats, or hitched rides in cattle cars. Others think they swam across the Mississippi. Scientists think the river is too deep and treacherous for them to swim across. However they managed to cross the river, armadillos continued their journey across the southern United States. In fact, nine-banded armadillos have ambled all the way east to the Atlantic Ocean. These shy creatures are natural survivors, and the story of their eastward migration shows how they **adapted,** or changed in order to fit into their environment. They changed their old ways and found new ways of living—learning to dig their burrows in new types of ground and to eat different kinds of food from those they had been accustomed to eating. Another reason armadillos were able to sweep across the southern states is that food was abundant and easy to find.

By the 1970s, nine-banded armadillos had reached the Florida Panhandle, in northwestern Florida. Eventually they joined up with the descendants of other armadillos that had escaped from a zoo. These armadillos had crept up from the Florida peninsula to the Panhandle.

Although nine-banded armadillos have wandered into Oklahoma, Kansas, Missouri, and Arkansas, cold weather limits their migration. When cold weather kills off surface insects, armadillos are forced to move on to warmer regions.

Because the armadillo, unlike most mammals, has no thick coat to keep it warm, and no extra layer of fat to help it wait out many days of very cold weather, it cannot keep warm enough for its body to function in cold climates. Only the insulating leaves and grass of the armadillo's nest allow it to survive the chill winters in northern **habitats** (the places where the animals live).

An armadillo's burrow is insulated with leaves and grass.

Armadillos do not **hibernate,** or pass the winter in a sluggish, inactive state, as some mammals do. For this reason, they need a source of food throughout the winter. The need for food often forces the animal to leave its burrow and become exposed to very low temperatures. A long spell of freezing weather has been known to wipe out entire armadillo populations. They must stay in warm climates to survive.

Unlike most mammals, the armadillo's body temperature does not remain constant. Its body heat goes up and down with the outside temperature. In summer, when the temperature may climb to over 100° F (38° C), armadillos have been known to breathe fast, flop over on their sides, and begin to pant in order to cool down.

To make up for their unusual body temperature feature, they have learned to avoid the heat of the day by staying inside their burrows till nightfall, when they emerge to look for food. But on cold winter days, armadillos venture out during the warmest part of the day, usually midafternoon. To help offset the cold, the armadillo shivers and crouches down or tucks its head under its belly. Still, the armadillo is better able to withstand extreme cold than extreme heat.

A nine-banded armadillo searches for food in the cool of the evening.

Armadillos not only burrow in the dirt for food and dig burrows to escape **predators,** or animals that kill and eat them, they also live part of their lives in burrows or dens and use them for breeding. Few animals of equal size have as many dens per animal as the armadillo. They can make their homes in many different kinds of habitats. They like warm climates and places with plenty of rainfall—enough to support the insects they eat and to supply water to drink. But their choice of a home is not only related to the climate and the presence of water, it also depends upon the soil.

Sandy, loose soils are especially good for burrowing. Because armadillos find their food by probing and scratching in the ground for insects and other forms of animal life, the texture of the soil during the dry season is extremely important. Hard-packed soils are harder to dig, and also make it harder for the animals to root for food with their long snouts.

Even in ideal sandy soil, danger is ever-present, for drought (a long period of time without rain) and flooding often kill armadillos. Drainage of water from the soil is important to these burrowing animals. If drainage of their sandy dens is poor, armadillos may drown during heavy rains. Sometimes, in marshy land, high water seeps into burrows and fills them.

In dry areas, armadillos choose to live near bodies of water. If a drought occurs, they follow the dry beds, searching for water. So the invasion route of the small pioneers generally runs parallel to water courses.

Armadillos like water. If the climate tends to be dry, the animals gather around streams and water holes. They are fond of small ponds, where they seek food and drink. Tracks around these ponds indicate that they also have a liking for mud baths.

In sandy soils, armadillos are extremely active diggers, and their burrows are found almost everywhere. In addition to those being lived in, many have been abandoned and are used only as temporary shelters. On coastal prairies, armadillos seek dens atop sandy knolls. They choose these small, rounded hills more for protection against floods than for ease of digging.

Armadillos make their homes in cracks and crevices of rocky outcroppings and rocky, unplowed fields. They like thickets and shrubby shaded areas of dense plant growth. Entrances to dens are often found at the base of trees and bushes with thick root systems, probably because these afford the best protection against enemies. If a growth of brush is cleared, or if the water supply dries up, armadillos will move on to colonize, or settle, another area.

Unlike their glyptodont ancestors, armadillos are good at adapting to new surroundings. They have colonized a variety of habitats, including ones that have been greatly changed by people and human activities. Armadillos often use golf courses and parks for digging dens, and homeowners' well-watered lawns and gardens for food gathering.

To dig their burrows, armadillos use the heavy claws on their front feet to scrape the dirt loose and push it back. With their hind legs, they toss the dirt out. The tail lifts the rear end so that the hind legs may kick more easily.

While digging a den, the armadillo has the unique ability to hold its breath for up to six minutes. This ability is helpful, for it allows the armadillo to dig for minutes at a time without uncovering its nose and mouth to breathe. To be able to dig quickly, without stopping to take a breath, is also useful when evading an enemy in close pursuit.

Right: *Armadillos, though timid, are not afraid to wander onto people's property when searching for food.* Opposite page: *An armadillo pushes its snout deep into the dirt as it digs its burrow.*

Armadillos usually occupy one burrow but have several burrows that they have abandoned and use only as emergency shelters or food traps. Most burrows have one entrance facing south, but burrows with as many as four entrances, each facing a different direction, have been found. Normally, each burrow is inhabited by only one adult armadillo, though other animals such as skunks, possums, burrowing owls, snakes, rabbits, rats, and minks have been found living in armadillo dens at times.

Burrows vary from 2 to 24 feet (60 cm-7.2 m) in length, and from a few inches below the ground to 5 feet (1.5 m) in depth. They are 7 to 8 inches (17.78-20.32 cm) wide. Nests open into a wider area, which the armadillo lines with leaves or grass. The burrow tunnel is usually fairly straight, with a few turns to avoid obstacles such as roots and rocks. Some tunnels may have two or more branches.

A nine-banded armadillo in its grass-lined nest

Shallow burrows with only one entrance often serve as food traps. Unsuspecting crickets, mosquitoes, beetles, or black widow spiders often take refuge inside the welcoming dark, damp den. Soon a keen-nosed armadillo sniffs out its prey. It wedges its stocky body against the walls and digs in with its claws to block the insect's escape. Then the hungry armadillo quickly devours its meal.

Burrows used for raising young usually have a special chamber or tunnel 18 inches or more in diameter with a slight turn in its downward slope to provide darkness for the young. The nest is lined with dried leaves, grasses, and twigs. The female collects this material and bunches it under her body. Then she stands on her hind legs and, clutching the dried material with her forepaws, hops backward to her burrow and nest chamber.

These two nine-banded armadillos are about to mate.

Armadillos have only one mate during each breeding season. Most females are more than a year old when they first mate. Older females **ovulate**, or produce eggs, earlier than younger females. During ovulation, the female releases one **ovum**, or egg. When a male and a female mate, this egg is fertilized. After mating, an unusual process takes place. The **embryo**, or fertilized egg, floats in the **uterus** (a hollow organ in the mother's body that holds the embryo during development) for four or more months. Then, usually in November, it attaches itself to the wall of the uterus.

Female nine-banded armadillos almost always give birth to four identical babies.

The nine-banded armadillo is one of the few North American mammals in which attachment of the fertilized egg to the uterus is delayed. In most mammals, the egg is attached to the uterus immediately after mating.

Once the egg is attached to the wall of the uterus, another unusual event occurs. The egg splits in half, then each half splits again, forming four separate embryos. The embryos develop into quadruplets, or four single babies, all of the same sex. Although other mammals produce quadruplets, the nine-banded armadillo is the only animal known to perform this remarkable feat on a routine basis.

The embryos' development period ranges from 120 to 150 days. In fact, growth of the embryo, or **gestation,** can sometimes take as long as 20 months. This seems a long time when you compare it with the average gestation period of other small mammals—for rabbits, 31 days; for cats, 63 days; for dogs, 61 days; for mice, 19 days; and for foxes, 52 days.

The litter is born in March or April. Some scientists think that the long wait before the fertilized egg is attached is one more way nine-banded armadillos adapt to their surroundings. This makes sense because if the birth of the babies were not put off until spring, they would be born during the winter, when food is scarce.

At birth, young armadillos are fully formed miniatures of their parents. Their eyes are open, and they can walk within a few hours. Their pale pink shells are soft at first, but within days, they turn brownish gray and begin to harden. The shells do not harden completely until the animal is fully grown.

Like all mammals, armadillos feed on their mothers' milk. After 2 months they are **weaned,** which means they give up feeding on their mothers' milk and accept other foods. After they are weaned, they stay with their mothers for several months. In the early evenings, they emerge from their dens to forage. The life span of armadillos in the wild is 7 to 10 years. The longest recorded life span for a captive armadillo is 16 years.

Armadillos have many natural enemies, such as coyotes, dogs, wildcats, wolves, and foxes. Coyotes and dogs are thought to be the chief killers of armadillos. But catching armadillos before they scuttle to safety in one of their many dens is no easy task.

When attacked by an enemy, the armadillo's first line of defense is to run away. With its gentle nature, and its habit of minding its own business, the armadillo would much rather run than fight.

If startled, it rises up on its hind feet and, balancing on its rat-like tail, sways this way and that, sniffing the warm air. Its keen sense of smell alerts it to danger. If it scents an enemy, it drops down on its short, stubby legs and takes off running.

This normally sluggish animal can put on an astonishing burst of speed over short distances, running a zigzag course like a football running back. If unable to outrun a predator, such as a dog, the armadillo stops and, forefeet flying, starts digging. The dog may snap at the odd creature, but its teeth slide off the leathery shell that covers the armadillo's back. Soil flies into the dog's face as the armadillo digs. The next minute, the animal buries itself inside its burrow. Bracing the bands of its back against the roof, it digs its claws into the sides. It is almost impossible to remove it, even by tugging on its tail. An armadillo can dig a new burrow and hide safely inside within two minutes.

Although the shell cannot protect the armadillo from the teeth of large animals, it is important because it enables the animal to plunge into dense brush or thickets where other animals can't penetrate. It can draw in its feet so that its armor touches the ground and duck its head so that even its eyes are protected by the shell, and only its ears are exposed. The shell also protects the armadillo from injury from sharp thorns or prickly cactus spines. If caught in the open, there is another way an armadillo can defend itself against an enemy. If all else fails, it will either stiffen, or totally relax and remain motionless, "playing dead."

A popular myth holds that when a nine-banded armadillo is attacked by an enemy, it will curl up into a tight ball to ward off attackers. It can pull its head inside its shell and curl its body so that head and tail meet (as in the large photograph at right), but it cannot roll into a ball. Only the South American three-banded armadillo can perform this feat (left).

There is one remarkable feat the nine-banded armadillo can perform—an unusual reflex it shares with the cat and the mule. When frightened or surprised, it can spring three feet into the air, lifting off like a rocket. Highway deaths are increased by the creature's unfortunate habit of jumping up when startled, when if it lay low, cars could pass over it. In fact, the greatest enemy of the armadillo is the car.

During the armadillo invasion at the turn of the century, armadillos were considered pests and were killed by the thousands. In those days, farmers and ranchers thought they ate eggs, fruits, and tomatoes, though later studies proved they ate mainly insects. The animals also left holes in the ground that were a hazard to farmers, animals, and horseback riders.

Cars, trucks, and other vehicles are the greatest enemies of armadillos, and dead armadillos (left) *are a common roadside sight in the areas where the animals live.*

People in many of the places where armadillos live celebrate the unusual creatures in different ways, including armadillo races in Orlando, Florida (right), *and Armadillo Day in Hamburg, Arkansas* (opposite page).

Nowadays some farmers feel that the holes the armadillos poke **aerate** the ground, allowing air to enter and dry it out or freshen it. Most agree that the little intruders eat many destructive insects and that they are helpful rather than harmful.

In the past 20 years, as people have come to know the armadillo better, their attitudes have changed. This small animal with the clumsy gait arouses the sympathy most people feel for the underdog. Nevertheless, because of their nighttime rambling, their snorting and grunting, their strong, musky odor, and their ability to claw out of pens, armadillos do not make good pets.

ARMADILLO DAY
1ST SAT. IN MAY
CARPENTER'S HOME SUPPLY

Scientists have discovered that the armadillo can make an important contribution to medical science. It is one of the only animals other than humans that can develop severe **leprosy,** or Hansen's disease. More than 13 million people suffer from this disease. Through their research with armadillos, scientists hope to find a vaccine to prevent leprosy.

Lepromin, a substance derived from armadillos infected with leprosy, enables doctors to determine how serious a case of leprosy a human patient will develop. A single armadillo provides enough material for more than one thousand units of lepromin.

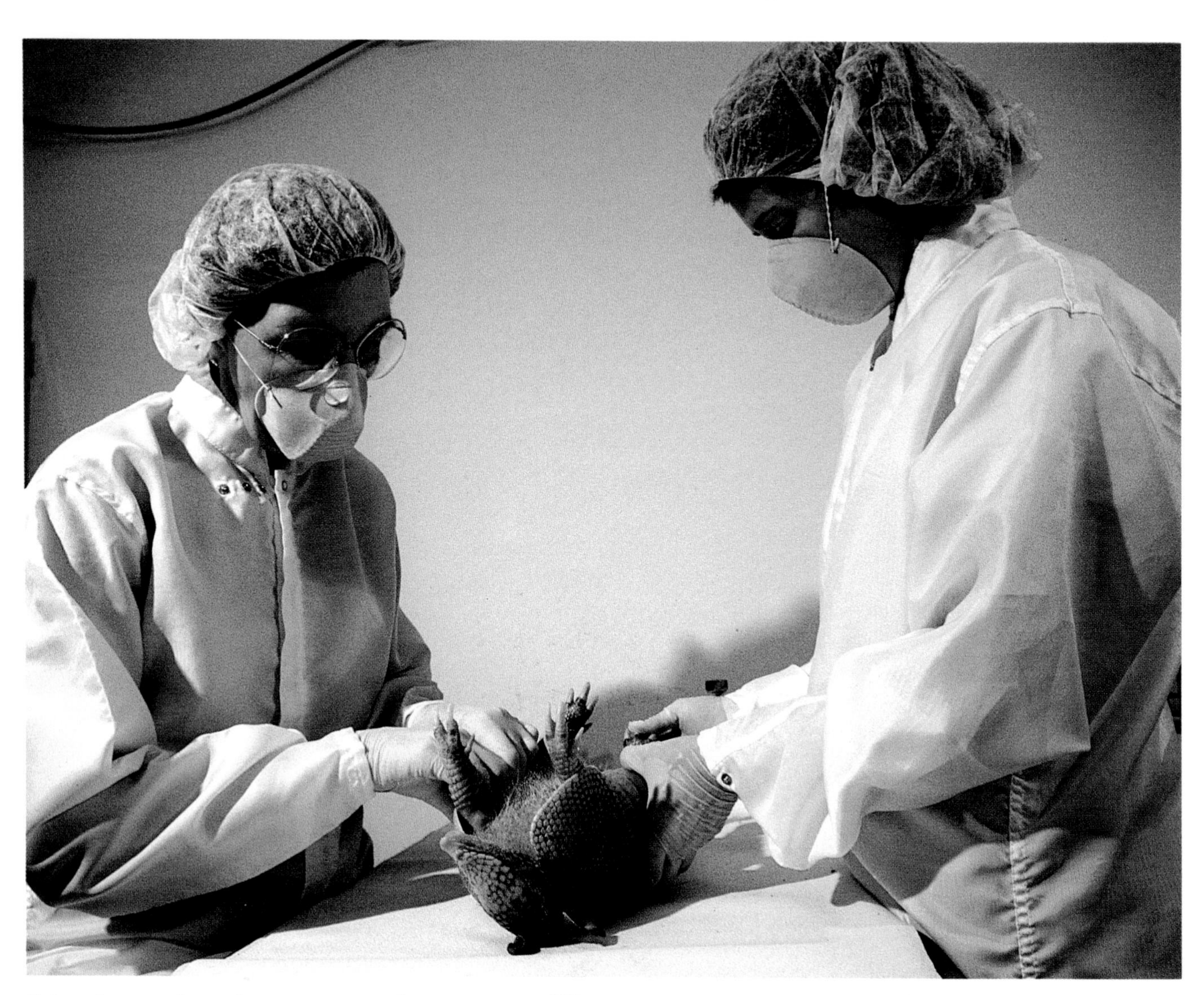

Scientists perform leprosy research on an armadillo.

The armadillo is one wildlife creature that is not an **endangered species** (a species in danger of dying out until it no longer exists). Biologists once thought that armadillos' enemies such as coyotes, wolves, wildcats, and some bears kept the number of armadillos down. But these scientists have discovered they were wrong. Although predators do sometimes kill them, recent studies have shown that very few predators feed on armadillos.

Other scientists thought that as human pioneers settled the lands and eliminated many predators, the armadillo population increased, and that in order to find enough food to survive, the animals were forced to spread out to new regions. But there is no hard evidence to show that the passing of these predators affected armadillo populations in either Mexico or Texas. As early as 1896, mammalogist Joel Asaph Allen found that when large predatory animals were widespread in South Texas, the armadillo population was increasing in the same area.

Why have these dauntless little survivors increased in number? They have adapted to warm temperatures by becoming mainly **nocturnal,** avoiding the heat of the day. They have learned to adapt to cold temperatures by staying inside their cozy burrows and venturing out only in the warmth of the sun. They have changed their diet, dining on whatever foods are available. They have trundled across woodlands and prairies, and have forded rivers and streams in search of suitable habitats. Finally, they have developed several ways to defend themselves against their enemies.

Today, tens of thousands of armadillos shuffle through the fields and woodlands of the southern United States. If you're out walking at dusk, and if you watch carefully, you may be lucky enough to see one of these timid, armored creatures that can be friends to people.

GLOSSARY

adapted: adjusted or changed to survive in an environment

aerate: to supply with air or oxygen

carapace: a protective case or shell on the back of an animal

colony: a group of settlers from another area

edentates: a group of related animals including anteaters, armadillos, and sloths

embryo: a living being in its earliest stages of development, as before birth

endangered species: a species in danger of dying out until it no longer exists

gestation: the development and carrying of offspring in the uterus

habitat: the area in which a plant or animal normally lives

hibernate: to pass the winter in a sleeping or resting state

larvae: the young of insects

lepromin: a substance produced by animals that have leprosy

leprosy: a serious disease caused by bacteria

maggots: the eggs of flies

migrate: moving from one country or region to settle in another

nocturnal: active during the night

ovulate: to produce or discharge eggs

ovum: the egg produced by a female mammal

predators: animals that destroy or kill and eat other animals

uterus: an organ in the female mammal that holds the fertilized egg during the development of the unborn young

weaned: able to give up mother's milk and eat food

Photo credits

Photographs courtesy of: p. 2, A.C. Harrison, Arkansas Department of Parks & Tourism; pp. 5, 7, 8, 11, 12, 19, 23, 24, 27, 28, 29, 32, 33, 36-37, 41, 42, 43, 44, front cover, back cover, © Jeff Foott; pp. 6, 10, 14, 15, 20, 21, 22, 25, 26, 30, 35, 36, 45, Jim Dunlap; pp. 18, 34, Stephen Kirkpatrick; p. 40, Florida Department of Commerce, Division of Tourism; pp. 31, 38, © Richard Stockton; p. 39, Texas Highways Magazine.

INDEX

ABOUT THE AUTHOR

A full-time writer and the author of numerous books for adults, **Dee Stuart** has always been fascinated by animals. After a foot-to-foot encounter with an armadillo in the Texas Hill Country, Ms. Stuart wanted to learn more about the odd little creature. Her research led her to write this book, her first book for children. Ms. Stuart has two children and three grandchildren. She lives with her husband in Richardson, Texas.